Houses

A ruined house, such as this ancient ferryman's cottage and farm across the river from Tintern Abbey, can be an interesting subject for study

Houses

Henry Pluckrose

Mills & Boon
ON LOCATION
Book no. 9

Drawings by Alec Davis
Photographs by Alec Davis and the
author

(Opposite)
An unusual plaque on a house in
Steyning, Sussex. The gentleman
named was a landlord with a
troublesome tenant who refused to
pay his rent and hoped to claim
ownership of the house. This plaque
was Sir Harry Gough's retaliation

MILLS & BOON Limited, London

First published in Great Britain 1974
by Mills & Boon Limited, 17-19 Foley
Street, London W1A IDR

© Henry Pluckrose 1974

ISBN 0 263 05580 9 (cased)
ISBN 0 263 05581 7 (limp)

Printed in Great Britain by
Biddles Ltd, Guildford, Surrey
Bound by Hunter & Foulis,
Edinburgh

Contents

A moated manor house (c. 1340) at Ightham, Kent

Preface

This little book is not a guide to the Englishman's home through the ages. Rather it is a book of clues — written for the young person who wants to know what to look for when visiting an old house (be the house a folk museum, the birthplace of a famous person, or the home of grandparents).

And yet I hope it will be used a little more widely than this. Our country is rich in houses, houses that reflect something of the life and customs of generations long since dead. We do not necessarily have to go into houses to trace their past. It is there for all who know how to look. If this book goes some way to helping you 'read' the houses you pass day by day as well as those you see for the first time on holiday or a school trip, then my writing it will have been worthwhile.

H.P.

1 Why houses?

If you were asked to make a list of the rooms that you would need if your family moved to a new house, I wonder how long the list would be? Certainly you would include rooms to sleep in, rooms to wash and cook in, and at least one room to 'live in'. Father might say that he needed a garage and a workshop as well as a shed and a greenhouse. Because you live in the second part of the twentieth century you would take certain things about this house for granted: that there would be a water supply, electricity points, gas for cooking, etc. You would want the house to be warm in the winter and dry in wet weather. You would also want it to be reasonably secure — with windows large enough to let in sunlight but strong enough to keep out burglars.

Now the interesting thing about this list is that your family needs are much the same as mine. Of course there will be slight differences. If my son takes up the trombone I might decide that a soundproof music room becomes a necessity; if you take in an elderly uncle who is confined to a wheelchair your family might have to install a special ground-floor toilet and bathroom. But because the list is essentially the same for you and me and the Jones family in Bradford and the Smith family in Taunton, it tells us something about the way we live in England *now*.

This is what makes the study of houses so worthwhile and so interesting. The farmworker of the fifteenth century would be amazed to hear your list of essentials: a toilet, a place to wash in, separate rooms to sleep in, piped water? Why, many of these things you couldn't even hope to find in the great Manor House!

Move on a few centuries. The craftsman living in York would question your list for other reasons. Separate bedrooms and living rooms he might approve of — but where was his storeroom and workshop? His house was his place of business. Indeed until the Industrial Revolution (c. 1780) most houses served more than one purpose (and many farmhouses still do). They were places for living, working and selling goods.

The Victorian gentleman would point out all the omissions in your

list. A house without servant quarters — unimaginable! There must be an attic for the maids and quarters in the semi-basement for the cook. The factory worker of the same period, living in a dingy street of back-to-back houses, sharing a toilet and one water pump with a dozen other families, would feel that both you and the Victorian gentleman lived in some world other than his.

So a house tells us something of the people who built it and of the times in which they lived. Sometimes we

Hall's Croft, the home of William Shakespeare's daughter, Susanna. This is the dispensary of Dr Hall, Susanna's husband. It contains apothecaries' jars for medicine, and a pestle and mortar for mixing and grinding. Most of the furniture and fittings in this room was hand-made — the nearer to our own time we get, the more likely we are to find that most things in a house have been mass-produced

have to delve for clues — for over the years the house may have been added to or altered or its use changed. Fortunately now and then we come across houses that have not altered overmuch: houses that have been deliberately preserved to show things as once they were. They might commemorate the life of a famous family or be used simply to show a style of living long since past (like the houses in the Open Museum at St Fagans, Cardiff). It is wise to try to visit some of these period houses before you look for clues in your own village or town. Once you have studied a few carefully preserved houses you will be better able to make informed comments upon houses you come across in your wanderings.

Having looked at a house and perhaps listened to the curator or owner tell something of its history, try to discover whether anyone has written anything about it.

(Above opposite)
Quebec House in Westerham, Kent, was where General Wolfe grew up. Why should it be called Quebec House?

(Below opposite)
Arms of John 'Butcher' Morley over the door of Blue Bridge House (built by him 1710-14), Halstead in Essex — an example of the ability of some tradesmen to rise in social class

One of the earliest stone-built dwelling houses in Europe; on Steep Hill, Lincoln

*An imposing sandstone house
fulfilling several purposes in Denton,
Northamptonshire — being farm,
manor and village house, situated at
the head of the village high street*

A staircase to nowhere, or was the window once a door? This house in Linton, Herefordshire, would be an ideal subject for some careful detection work

Some local research can be very worthwhile in helping make the building come alive.

Finally, remember that our houses in the British Isles also reflect our climate, which is damp and mild. The homes of the British have had to cope with rain and wind, fog, frost and snow and long warm summer days. But they have never had to be built to stand long periods of intense cold or intense heat. If ever you go abroad look at the houses. They will tell you something of the customs and life style of the people who live in them. They will also tell you something about their climate.

A lake dwelling. Did the houses of Glastonbury look like this?

2 How houses developed

Before looking at houses in greater detail, think for a moment of how you would go about building a house from scratch. You have a site — and that's all. The materials are around you: wood, hunks of stone, reeds, rushes and clay. What materials would you use where? Would the house be long and low or tall and square? This was the sort of problem facing the leaders of the early Britons when they stopped being nomadic and began to farm a particular piece of countryside. To farm successfully they had to settle in one place — and settling meant building a place that gave protection from the worst of the weather as well as protection from dangerous animals and strangers from other tribes.

Archaeologists know that the early tribes in Britain made at least two different types of settlement. Near Glastonbury in Somerset, for example, a lake village has been excavated. The houses were built on a foundation of poles and small tree trunks. So close together were the houses that an island was formed in the middle of the lake. As wood was plentiful and easy to work it was the obvious material to use. Mud filled the gaps in the buildings and a thick thatch kept out the rain. But wood rots, and apart from bracelets, rings, pots and a dugout canoe in the Glastonbury Museum there is little for us to see of the actual houses of the Bronze Age folk who lived on the lake.

In Cornwall, however, stone is more plentiful than wood, so it's not surprising to find that the houses that have been excavated at Chysauster had stone walls. Each house was circular (which made it easier to build with small stones) and opened onto a central courtyard. The roof was probably thatched. We also know that each householder had his own stone-walled back garden. The remains of a similar stone village can be seen at Din Lligwy, near Holyhead in Anglesey, although here some of the houses were built to a more rectangular design.

We also have archaeological evidence of the sort of houses that wealthy Romans lived in, but because these villas are not really typical of the homes of ordinary folk, I won't include them here. However it is worth noting that the Romans used

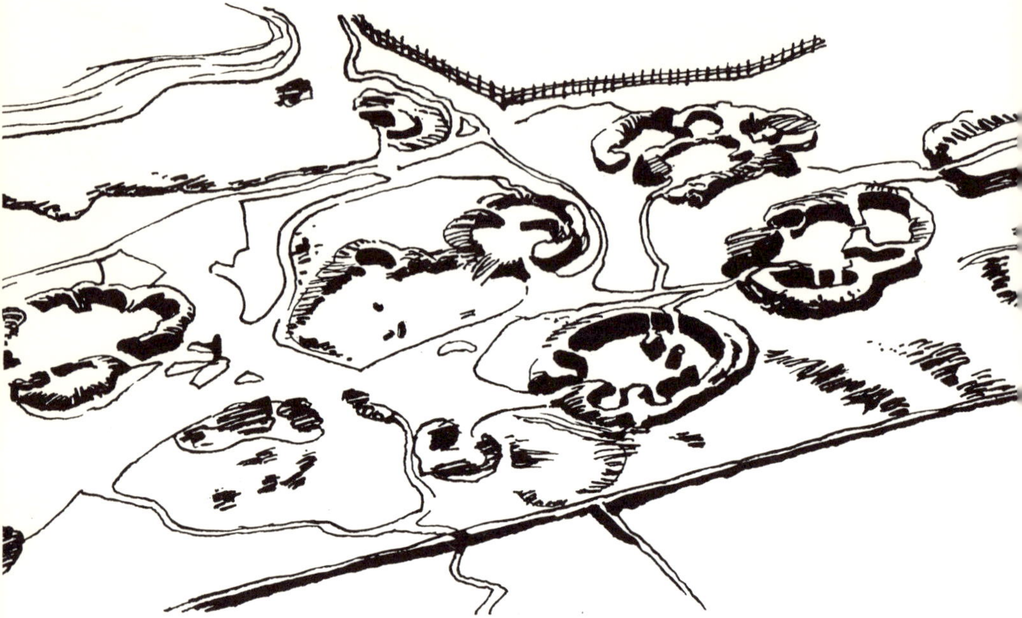

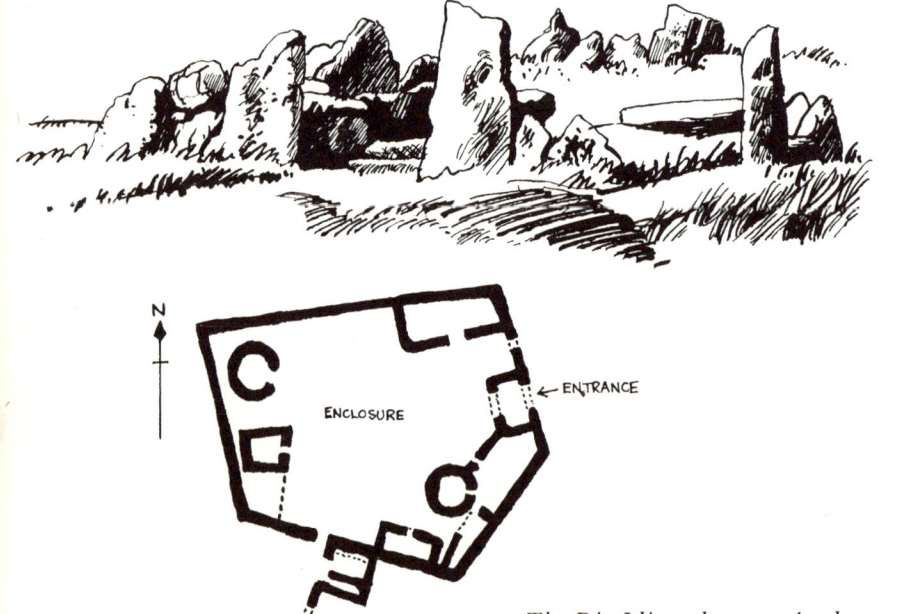

Aerial view of Chysauster Village, Cornwall

ENCLOSURE

← ENTRANCE

The Din Lligwy huts on Anglesey

cut and shaped stone, made and decorated their own tiles from clay, fashioned water pipes from lead and leather, paved courtyards and built walls around their gardens. They not only took the raw materials that were available; they treated the raw materials in such a way as to make their dwellings more comfortable (just as we do today).

The Romans finally left Britain in AD 410 and there is little architectural evidence of the centuries that followed. We know that the Saxons built mainly in wood, although some of their stone churches remain. Even when the Normans came wood was still the main building material, stone being reserved for some of the more important castles and churches (see *On Location: Castles* and *On Location: Churches*).

Central heating is not a modern invention. Under the famous mosaic floors of the Roman villa at Bignor in Sussex lies this hypocaust through which a draught of hot air flowed

It is likely, however, that the **cruck house** spans these centuries that we know so little about. Certainly excavations in Lincolnshire and Sussex (both in 1968) suggest that the cruck house was common right across Britain. How did this building style develop?

Naturally bent timbers were used to form the cruck

Remember that Britain was covered with forests. All that was needed was to find trees that were gently curved. The tree, usually an oak, was cut down and trimmed. The trunk was then sawn along its length. A sawpit was used for this, the housewright (builder) working above and his assistant below. The assistant was known as the 'underdog'. Can you think why? The two halves of each trunk formed one cruck.

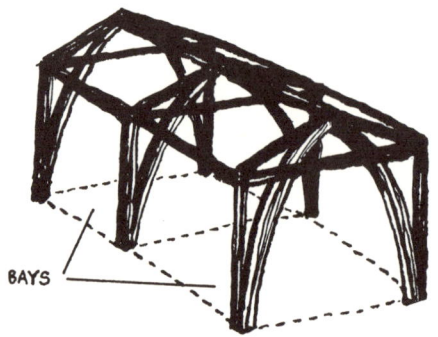

The cruck was the base for additional timber framing. A long building would be built in this way, with the roof supported on pairs of crucks throughout its length; the space between each pair of crucks was called a bay

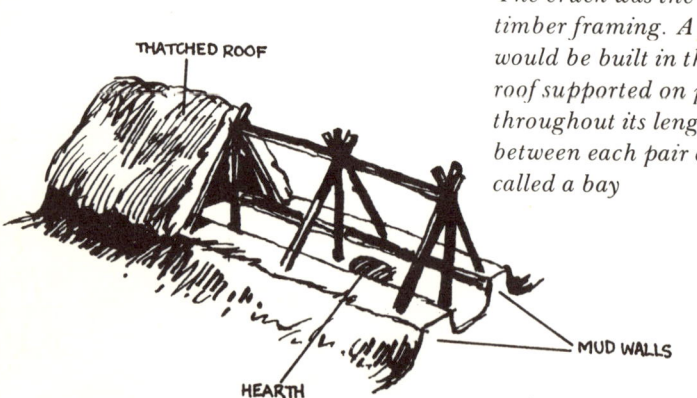

A primitive cruck dwelling with the floor cut away to give greater height and support to the roof

But wood rots if placed directly onto the ground. Some early builders charred the ends of each cruck to slow down decay. Eventually it was found that if the crucks were set in a wall of stones above ground level, the wood rotted much more slowly and more height was given to the inside of the house.

be the easiest place to add a chimney piece — on an end wall or through the centre of the building?

Nowadays cruck houses have all manner of fillings between the beams. See how many different types of filling you can discover.

As timber suitable for making crucks became more scarce, houses were built around simple box frames. This style of building was practised until late Stuart times. Of course the later buildings were more sophisticated than the earlier ones, with rooms on the first floor, built-in chimney stacks and quite elaborate kitchens.

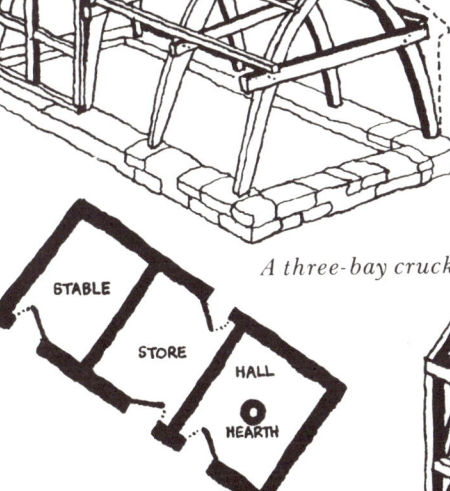

A three-bay cruck

The first cruck houses (these are sometimes called cruck-truss constructions) would have had a central hearth with a hole in the roof to let out the smoke. It was not until a first floor was needed to give extra accommodation that fireplaces and chimney stacks were added. If the house was already built, where would

A timber-framed house

(Opposite)
A cruck house in Ledbury,
Herefordshire

Frame house being renovated in
Suffolk

A stone chimney was often added to the outside of a timber-framed house, as to this one in Fownhope, Herefordshire

It's worth trying to discover who lived in the houses you visit. Sometimes its name (or the name of the street in which it stands) provides a clue. The small timber-framed house and the cruck house were often 'yeoman's houses' (a yeoman was a freeholder of land that had a rental value of 40/- or more a year) belonging to a weaver, a glover, a miller or a housewright. The size of the house will indicate the importance of past owners. Thomas Hardy's cottage, Upper Bothenhampton in Dorset, was a 'Yeoman's holding'. It has seven rooms and a garden.

In each mediaeval village there was also the Lord's Hall or Manor House — built in stone or in timber framing. Even if stone were used throughout, its shape was very similar to the neighbouring houses,

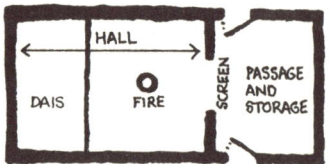

The manor house — a basic plan

which were built in wood, wattle and daub. The manor house gave privacy to the Lord's family, and it was a much larger dwelling, often being protected by a moat and having its own chapel. Notice that the hall was the centrepiece of the dwelling. How does this compare with the hall in the house in which you live?

(Opposite)
Box-framed weaver's cottage in Lavenham, Suffolk. Notice the large windows to give extra working light

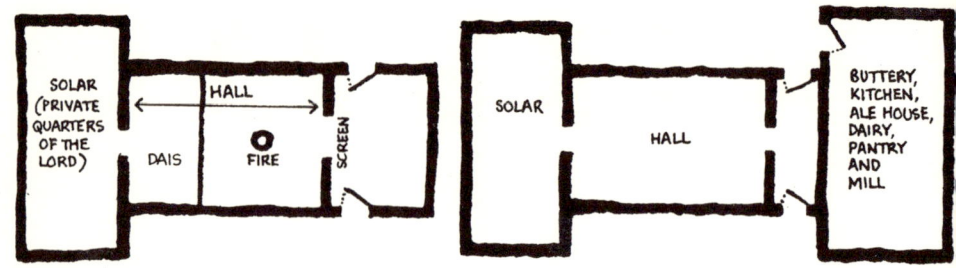

Extension for the Lord . . .

. . . and for the servants.
Look at the pictures and plans that
follow and notice the similarities to
the simple development shown here

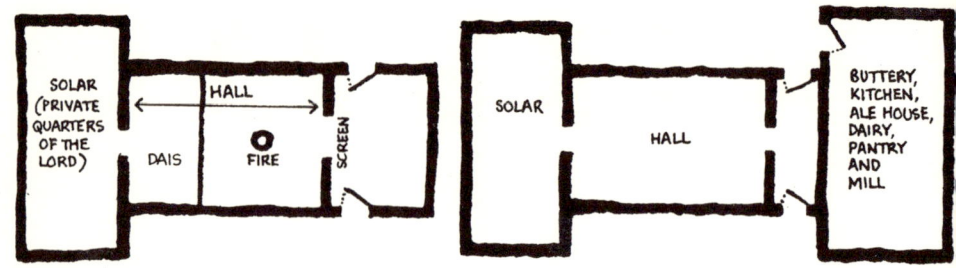

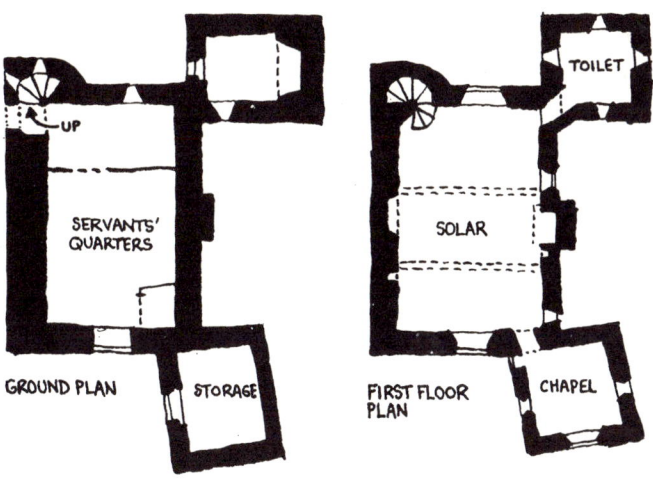

Old Soar Manor, Plaxtol, Kent
(c. 1290). Here the house is on two
floors: the room beneath the chapel
for storage, the one beneath the solar
for servants' quarters

(Photograph opposite)
Old Soar Manor today

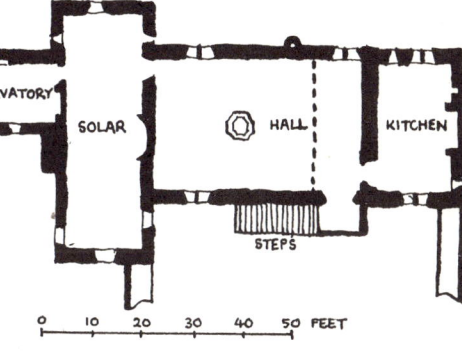

Manor house from the time of
Edward I, c. 1300

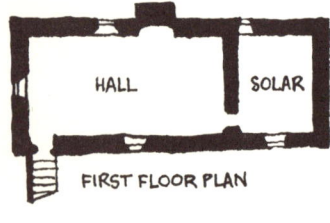

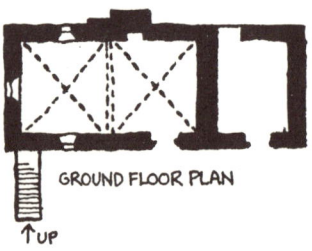

*Boothby Pagnell Manor,
Lincolnshire, built c. 1180. The
lower rooms are vaulted and were
used for storage. An easily defended
stairway leads to the living quarters*

*Manor house from the reign of
Richard III, c. 1480
Plan above opposite*

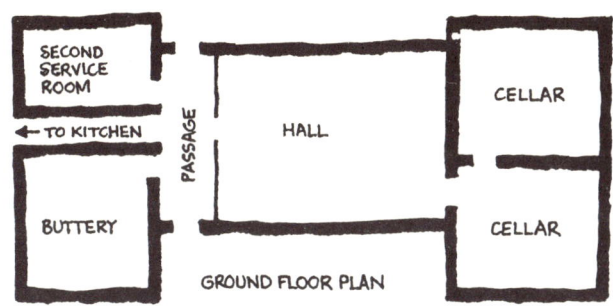

GROUND FLOOR PLAN

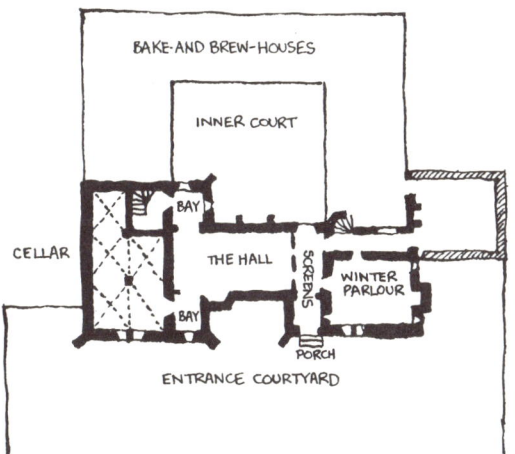

(Left) A manor house built about 1490. Notice that the Great Hall still exists, but takes up a smaller proportion of the building than before

The screens passage in Fir Tree Farm, Forncett St Mary, Norfolk. On the left is the doorway to the hall, on the right two doorways to the kitchen. A screens passage was a passage screening or dividing the kitchen from the hall; in early Tudor halls the minstrels' gallery was situated over the screens

So far we have considered houses whose construction was based upon a wooden frame. Many of these houses have survived, but it would be wrong to think that houses of this type were lived in by the majority of the population. Indeed outside the great mediaeval towns (e.g. Norwich, London, Chester, York) most people would have been content to live in little more than a hovel.

The mediaeval town house (many of which have been preserved) was built upwards rather than outwards so that as many dwellings as possible could be fitted within the town walls. The houses were jettied so that although the base (ground floor) was small, the various overhanging stories gave the maximum living space. Cellars were also common. These houses usually had a very narrow frontage onto the road but were deep from front to back. Along the back of the houses

(Opposite)
Jettied houses in Lavenham, Suffolk

The Merchant's House in Yarmouth, Norfolk (c. 1600) and a 'row' alongside

(Opposite)
Abbot's Lodge in Ledbury,
Herefordshire, has a jettied bay
window forming a porch over the
door

The Shambles — a narrow street of
jettied Tudor houses in York

there was often a narrow lane. These lanes had different names in different parts of the country. In Yarmouth they were known as 'rows', in Edinburgh 'wynds' and 'closes', and in some northern towns simply 'the backs'. These names are still in use.

It's worth noting that although most of the timber houses we see today are painted white with black beams, in mediaeval times the wood was left to weather naturally. The facing between the beams (see pages 43-4) would have been orange. This colour, known as minium, was made from lead. Other colours available were cinnabar (browny-red) made from mercuric sulphide; rose madder (deep pink) made from the root of the madder plant, and orpiment (yellow) made from arsenic. The only trouble with these paints was that they were poisonous and faded quickly.

As towns began to be rebuilt (sometimes after great fires like that which devastated London in 1666), brick and stone began to replace wood. James I of England, who came from Scotland where stone-built houses were far more common than timber ones, wanted a London of 'bricks rather than sticks'. Although Oliver Cromwell did try to encourage planned house building (the first planned terrace houses were built during the Protectorate on the estate of the Duke of Bedford in London by

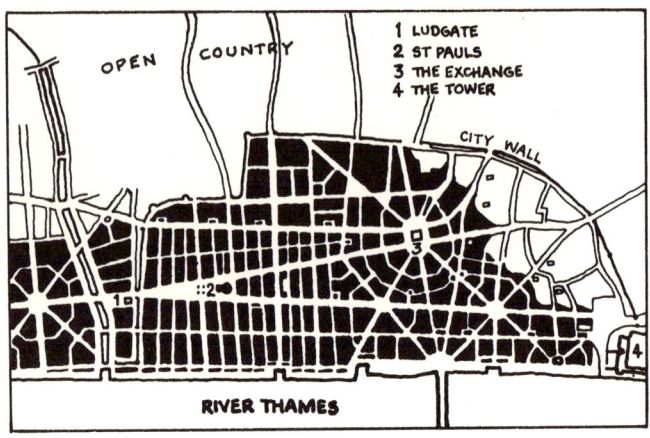

Wren's map for London after the Great Fire

Praise-God Barebones), it was the Great Fire that encouraged architects to think of houses as part of a street, a square or a crescent.

The two great architects of this period were Inigo Jones (1573-1652) and Christopher Wren (1632-1723).

Like architects on the continent of Europe, Jones and Wren began to look at the ruined buildings of ancient Greece and Rome, and attempted to blend some of the beauty of these earlier civilizations into their own work. This rebirth (or renaissance) of an older style can be seen in the houses of the period.

The Queen's House, Greenwich, designed by Inigo Jones. Compare this with the timber-framed houses of the same period

*A Renaissance-style town house in
Lincoln's Inn Fields, London*

Architects who followed, the most famous of whom was Robert Adam (1728-92), tried to make their houses places that were beautiful to look at and beautiful to live in. Great care was taken to ensure that windows in each wall 'balanced'; that fittings (such as door handles and window catches) blended in with the woodwork; that the woodwork itself harmonized with the walls. At this time soft woods were more readily available than they had been hitherto, which enabled much finer decoration to be attempted on all wooden surfaces. Of course houses of this type — often built in a combination of brick and stone — were not available for any but the comfortably rich, but the ideas were copied by lesser architects and incorporated into many houses of the period.

A Georgian house in Abbey Street, Bath

John Nash (1752-1835) lived at a time when the population was increasing rapidly and more people, because of industrialization, needed to live in towns. If houses could be built in a long terrace (each house being joined to its neighbour), it would be possible to have an attractive building to look at — even if each of the houses that made up the building was, in itself, quite small.

This period (1700-1800) also saw the development of towns that were 'spas'. These were health centres where it was possible to bathe in local waters that were thought to have special medicinal properties. Cheltenham, Glastonbury, Harrogate, Tonbridge and Leamington each had their springs; but the most famous spa was Bath. Inspired by John Wood (1704-54),

Bath was laid out in squares and crescents, straight roads crossing each other at a grass-covered circus. Again an attempt was made to plan each house so that it blended with its neighbour.

So we come to the age of coal and steel and steam. The factories that were springing up needed men and women to work in them — and the men and women needed somewhere to live. The simplest thing to do was to build houses near the factories and to build the houses close together so that as many people as possible could be housed near their work. If the houses were built back to back with each front door opening directly onto the street, space would be saved — for more houses! Many industrial towns developed in this way and some of the workers' tiny 'cottages' are still to be seen. These houses were poor places to live in. The water supply was often no more than a pump in the middle of the street, toilets were shared by perhaps a dozen families and the accommodation was very cramped. There were no open spaces for children to play in. In these conditions disease (particularly cholera) spread rapidly.

Industrial back-to-back houses built before 1840 in Preston, Lancashire. The houses were built next to the cotton mill, but although they were in open country-side, they were still crowded together. Sewage from the open toilets flowed into the central cesspool

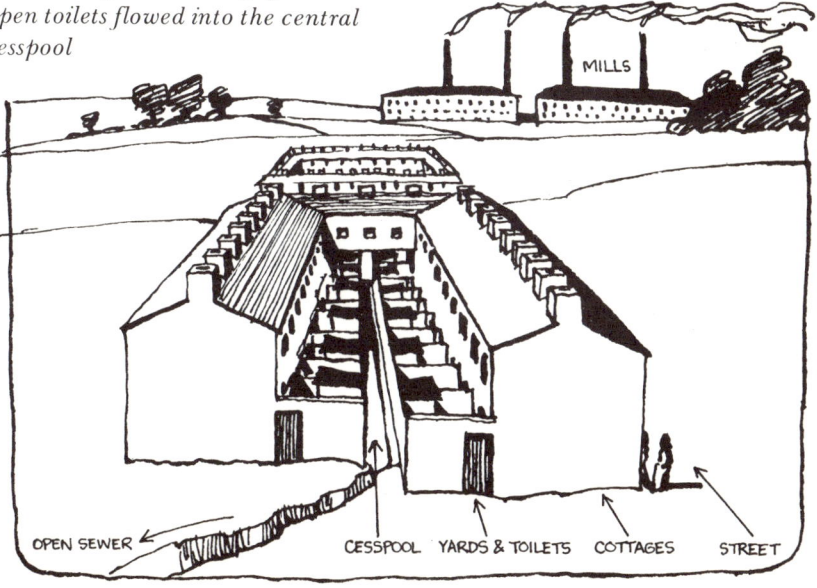

OPEN SEWER   CESSPOOL   YARDS & TOILETS   COTTAGES   STREET   MILLS

(Opposite)
'Bluegate Fields', an engraving by
Gustave Doré, reproduced by
permission of the Mansell Collection

Industrial houses in
Newcastle-upon-Tyne. The front
doors are in pairs: one for the
downstairs house, the other for the
upstairs house

But some workers were more fortunate. At Chippenham in Cambridgeshire the squire built a complete village — 'Squires village' — for the workers on his estate. In New Lanark Robert Owen built a village for his mill hands, even including a school. In Sheffield the steel workers of Abbeydale had a cottage and a walled garden. If you are particularly interested in this period of history, try to discover if there were any developments of this sort in the area in which you live.

In Victorian times there was a return to a building style of a previous age: a style sometimes known as 'Sham Gothic'. Doors and windows were arched (like a church), the walls

*A Victorian suburban villa of the
1860s. How many 'styles' can you see
in this one house?*

given battlements, towers and
pinnacles (like a castle). It's
interesting to note how often house
builders return to the past for their
inspiration. How many
advertisements for modern 'Georgian
Houses' can you find in your local
paper?

Few of the houses that we have
considered so far were
semi-detached. They were either
completely detached or built in rows.
Trinity Street, Weymouth (Dorset),
is said to contain the earliest pair of
purpose built semi-detached houses
in the country — and these date from
the middle of the nineteenth century.
Nowadays, when most families have
cars, semi-detached houses are very
popular. Can you think why?

Towns, then, provide much valuable
material for any study of houses. The
centre of the town (unless it has been
torn apart by developers) may have
mediaeval associations. Around this
core, running in bands outwards
from the centre, look for
developments made by builders in

Georgian, Victorian and modern times. The town of Stamford in Lincolnshire illustrates this growth pattern. The earliest domestic building dates from 1450 (William Brown's almshouses) and there are good examples of Tudor, Stuart, Queen Anne, Georgian, Victorian and modern architecture. At one time there were seventeen churches in the town and many of the houses are built over the crypts, passageways and cellars of far older buildings.

Try dating the buildings in your town or city. Where are the oldest houses? Where are the Georgian houses? Where are the Victorian houses? Plot your findings on a street plan. Does this tell you anything about how your town developed? One word of caution before you begin. Remember that just as the styles of buildings change over the centuries so does their function. The building may have been altered to meet a changing need. Outhouses may have been built onto an existing building, two separate buildings joined to make one, or a shop front added. Because a building is no longer a house (being now a shop or an office) does not mean that it never was one once.

(Opposite)
Such a mediaeval street as this one in Ledbury, Herefordshire, will yield much valuable information for a study of houses

The growth pattern of a town (see page 39) is not always a gradual one — these days, whole areas of old houses can be torn down for the building of a new estate, like this one in London

3 What to look for —outside

Before we examine the smaller objects that will tell us something of the history of a house, let us look first at its principal parts: the walls, the roof, the chimneys, the windows and the doors. The questions that follow can be applied equally well to a Tudor cottage or a house on a modern council estate.

The walls

Does the wooden timbering provide the basic structure?
If so, what other material has been used? In Chapter 2 we saw that wood

Tower Hill House in Bromyard, Herefordshire, dated 1630, has varying lozenge designs and a two-storey porch

was a common building material
because it was plentiful and easy to
work. But if stout wooden beams
provide the framework how have the
spaces between the timbers been
filled?

*Wattle frame between timber
supports*

Has wattle and daub been used?
Wattle panels were made from
upright stakes of hazel, willow or oak
woven with hazel wands (known as
osiers). These panels were first fixed
between the timber frame and then
filled. The filling consisted of clay or
cow dung mixed with straw or animal
hair. When dry a coat of lime plaster
or whitewash completed the wall.

Has the wattle been plastered?
The plaster was a mixture of lime
and sand mixed with cow hair.

*Pargeting on 'Cromwell's House'
(actually an old inn), in Saffron
Walden, Essex*

**Has the filling any local
characteristics?** For example, in
Devon and Dorset the cottages are
known as 'cob cottages'. Here mud
and chippings were mixed with straw
and farmyard dung. Where
farmyard dung was not plentiful
mud, sand, leaf mould and clay were
strengthened with chopped straw.
'Cob' is very porous. To keep these
cottages dry they were built on stone
foundations and given an
overhanging thatched roof — for a
cob cottage needs 'a wide hat and
stout shoes'. In the north-west
Midlands, the combination of close
timbering and even infilling is called
'Magpie'. Can you think why?

*A timber-faced cottage in Heybridge
Basin, Essex*

Is the daub and plaster decorated?
Usually this was done to break up the
flow of rainwater. This decoration,
known as pargeting, can be
extremely ornate. The pargeter (the
craftsman who decorated the house)
often dated his work, but remember
that this may only tell us when his
work was done, not the date the
house was built.

**Have bricks been used for the
infilling** (known as brick nogging)?
How have the bricks been
arranged — horizontally, vertically or
diagonally? Which type of filling
gives the greatest strength?

Is the house timber faced? In parts
of south-east England many houses
are entirely faced with wood, the
planks being pinned horizontally to

the frame. This is known as
weatherboarding or clapboarding.
Sometimes the edges of the planks
were left untrimmed to give
additional pattern to the building.
Occasionally weatherboarding
simply indicates that the original
daub and wattle were not waterproof
and had, at some time, to be
reinforced or replaced.

**Is the wall on which the frame
stands of brick or stone? Is the
house faced with tile?** Tile
making had gone out of practice
during the late thirteenth century,
but revived when a tax was imposed
on bricks in 1784. (The tax was
repealed in 1850.) What shape are
the tiles? What patterns do they
make?

Brick infilling in herringbone pattern, Lavenham in Suffolk (above)

Tile facing, near Crowborough in Kent (below)

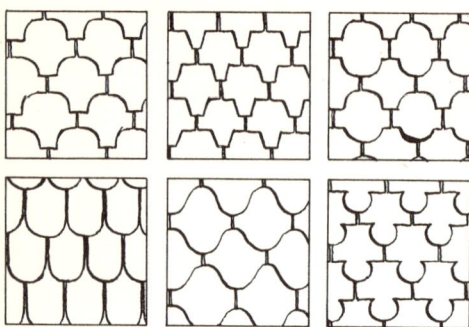

Typical tile decorations

The Tribunal, Glastonbury in Somerset. Look at the size and shape of the stones

Are the walls made of stone?
England's first quarry was opened near Bath, probably by St Aldhelm (640-709). Aldhelm, who built the famous Saxon church at Bradford, Wiltshire, brought masons from the continent to work the stone. The use of stone for building spread across those parts of England where stone was easily obtainable: Warwickshire, Oxfordshire, Wiltshire, Gloucestershire, Worcestershire, Northamptonshire, and Yorkshire., On Dartmoor and across Cornwall 'moor stones', found in outcrops of granite, provided the only natural building material in an area where wood was far from plentiful. Stone houses, many quite old, are found in parts of the country where rebellion and armed raids were once common — particularly the border counties of England, Scotland and Wales.

What stone is used? Where is it quarried? Is the use of the stone common throughout the area? Does the stone give a pattern to the buildings in the area? Try to find out something about local stone by arranging a visit to a quarry, but *never* explore a working or even an old one without seeking permission from the owner and without being accompanied by an experienced guide.

(Opposite)
Compare these stones with the regular shape of 'dressed' stone. A house near Stirling in Scotland

Is stone used throughout? Or simply for quoins and door and window architraves? What other materials have been used with the stone?

Has the stone been faced or shaped (i.e. smoothed) or has it been used 'rough cut'?

Have the walls been rendered? Rendering is a covering of a wash (lime-sand) to give greater protection against the weather.

Are the walls made of cobbles or pebbles? Being rounded, these are difficult materials to build in. Walls of cobble stone are found in areas that are poor in other building materials. How are the cobbles laid? What other materials are used to reinforce the cobbles? Have the

Stone quoins, knapped flint, pebbles and even whale bones (in the decoration below roof) are all to be found in this house in Cley, Norfolk

cobbles been rendered? What material has been used? Along the coasts, look for tarred cobbled walls.

Are the walls made of flint? As with cobbles, flint is difficult to use without the addition of some other building material (particularly at corners). What pattern does the flint make? Has the flint been knapped (i.e. cut to give a smooth face) or is it used 'rough'? What other materials have been used to reinforce the flint?

Are the walls made of brick? The oldest existing brick manor house was built at Little Wenham, Suffolk, in about 1280, so we are unlikely to find a brick-built house of an earlier date! Brick was first brought to England as ballast for ships but in the late Middle Ages bricks were made from local clay. They were smaller than those we use today (4½" x 4½" x 2") and poorly made, being fired in open kilns (clamps). As a result mediaeval bricks are found in a variety of sizes and colours (red, brown, black, red, yellow).

ENGLISH BONDING   FLEMISH BONDING

DIAMOND DIAPERING

How are the bricks laid? Before the Flemings came to live in England, English bond was common. This meant laying bricks in alternate layers of headers and stretchers. A 'stretcher' is a brick laid so that its side is showing, a 'header' is a brick laid so that only its end is showing. To escape religious persecution, the Flemings settled in England during late Tudor times. They introduced Flemish bond: headers and stretchers laid alternately in each course of bricks. Does this help you date the house? Have bricks of different colours been used to make a regular pattern? This is called diapering.

The roof

What sort of roof does the house have? There are only two types of roof: the hipped roof and the gabled roof. The hipped roof slopes in from all sides of the building; the gabled roof slopes from two opposite sides, the end walls going upwards beyond the eaves.

Roof shapes

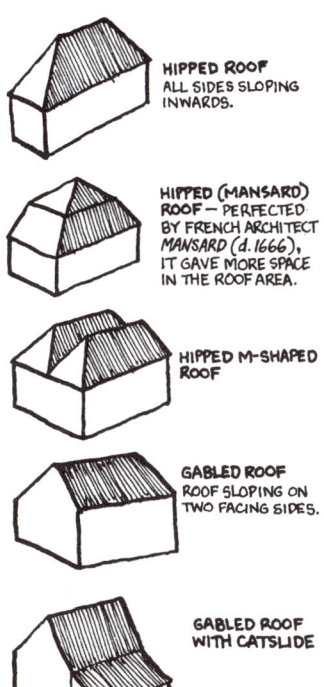

HIPPED ROOF
ALL SIDES SLOPING INWARDS.

HIPPED (MANSARD) ROOF — PERFECTED BY FRENCH ARCHITECT MANSARD (d.1666), IT GAVE MORE SPACE IN THE ROOF AREA.

HIPPED M-SHAPED ROOF

GABLED ROOF
ROOF SLOPING ON TWO FACING SIDES.

GABLED ROOF WITH CATSLIDE

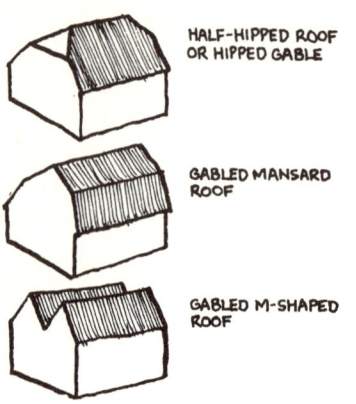

HALF-HIPPED ROOF
OR HIPPED GABLE

GABLED MANSARD
ROOF

GABLED M-SHAPED
ROOF

What roof covering has been used?

Reed or thatch is to be found in most parts of Britain. Even in Wales, where easily obtainable slate is widely used, thatched cottages are not uncommon. Materials most suitable for thatch are reed, rush, broom, and heather, and straw from barley,

Stone roof, Worth Matravers in Dorset. The largest stone tiles are along the eaves of the building

Plain tiles (notice the slight camber in each hand-made tile) and pantiles

A thatcher using a wooden 'bat' to drive home the Norfolk reeds. A large cottage roof takes him about eight weeks

Thatching details, near Corfe in Dorset

A thatched cottage in Denton, Northamptonshire, with a pattern of 'sways' (hazel spars) at the apex of the roof

wheat and rye. Has the thatch been finished with a pattern, a model animal or bird?

A KNEELER

Look at the slope of the roof. If the house is stone roofed, does the roof have a steep or a low pitch? If the house is tiled does the roof have a steep or low pitch? What will the slope of the roof tell us about the quality of the roofing material?

What decorations can you see along the eaves? Is there a parapet (common in many Georgian houses) or a decorated cornice?

DUTCH GABLE

What decorations can you see along the gable? Is there a a parapet? Is there a Dutch gable? If so, is this style common to many houses in the area? (The Flemings tended to settle in the east of England.) Is there an interestingly shaped kneeler or carved bargeboarding?

COW STEPS

Carved oak bargeboarding in Sussex

The chimney

The easiest place to build a chimney was against an outside wall; many mediaeval builders overcame the problem of taking a chimney stack up through the roof by adding an external chimney breast. The position of a chimney breast will help date a house, provided, of course, that there is other supporting evidence. Fireplaces on end walls are not economic (a lot of heat is lost) and in the early seventeenth century the stack was brought inside and placed centrally to carry more than one fireplace.

Where is the chimney? Does it project from the ground floor on the gable or side wall of the house? At what level (ground or first floor)? What do you think the ground floor might have been used for originally if the main heating was on first-floor level? Is the chimney within the house, at a gable end, in the centre projecting through the ridge or through some other part of the roof?

What materials have been used for the stack and chimneys? Is there any decoration?

Chimneys: from the left, mid-seventeenth century, seventeenth century, thirteenth century, fourteenth century modelled chimney cover

Chimney positions

*Decorated Tudor chimneys at
Denver in Northamptonshire*

*A pottery louver or smoke vent
(c.1300-25). Now in Saffron Walden
Museum, Essex, it was once fitted in
the roof above the open centre hearth
in a great hall*

The windows

Window comes from the words 'wind eye', a hole in the wall for ventilation and for looking through. The very earliest 'wind eyes' were probably covered with a lattice of twigs woven diagonally. This helped keep out the rain, the diamond pattern causing the water to run downwards and outwards, so preventing too many drips from coming inside.

Tudor lattice window

What shape are the windows? Look for diamond lattice work in the window leads of old houses. The folk-pattern continues, even though the reason for the pattern no longer applies. As glass became cheaper and larger panes could be made, windows become a more prominent feature of domestic architecture.

What material is used for the framework? (stone, lead, wood). Is there any evidence that shutters were once used?

Have any of the windows been bricked in? In 1697 a window tax was imposed upon the owners of houses that had more than six windows and a rental value of £5 or more. There was a sliding scale:

Fewer than 10 windows tax 2/- per year

9-19 windows tax 6/- per year

Over 20 windows tax 10/- per year

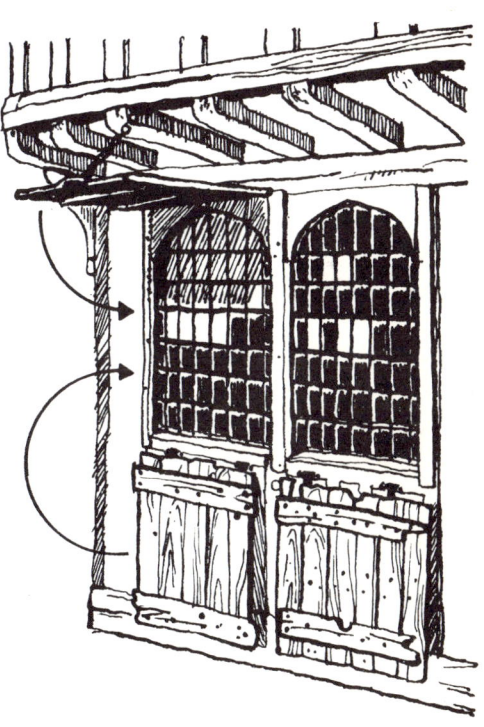

Timber shutters in Lavenham, Suffolk

EARLY ENGLISH

1400

TUDOR

WOODEN MULLION

STONE FRAME WITH IRON BARS

TUDOR

RENAISSANCE

GEORGIAN

REGENCY

QUEEN ANNE

NOW

Window development

The tax resulted in people blocking in windows they felt they could do without. It was repealed in 1851. Thus if a house has windows filled in, it was built before 1851 — and may have been built before 1697.

Queen Anne period window canopy shaped like a shell. Similar canopies were built over doors

A dormer window breaks into the roof above the line of the eaves

A 'Venetian' window (left)

MANOR HOUSE

*A manor house in Gloucestershire
with 17th century windows
surmounted by 'dripstones', built to
divert rain running down the walls
from the windows*

*Notice the planned proportions of
the windows of this late 18th century
terrace in London, reducing in
height with each additional storey*

*A Queen Anne bow window in
Maldon, Essex. (By the way, how
many different kinds of windows can
you see reflected in the glass?)*

**Did any of the windows serve some
specific purpose?** In the Yorkshire
villages of Golcar, Delph and
Dobcross many of the houses have a
continuous line of windows across the
upper storey so the weavers'
workshops would be as well lit as
possible. Hardy's Cottage (Upper
Bothenhampton, Dorset) has a wages
window through which the workmen
employed by the Hardy family could
be paid (it kept dirty boots from the
house).

*A doorway in Lavenham, Suffolk.
From the drawings on pages 66-7
can you guess its age?*

The doorway

A brief examination of the doorway
may give additional information
about the house. What shape is it?
How wide is it? Some mediaeval
doors are much wider than those we
use today, probably because they
were used by animals as well as
humans. Is the door on ground,
basement or first-floor level? **Does the
door** hang within a doorframe or
from the actual structure of the
building? Is there any door-furniture
of interest? e.g. hinges, knockers,
locks. Look for decoration around
the doorframe. Are there any dates
or inscriptions?

*An item of door furniture — an iron
shoe scraper*

Fincham Hall, Northants., features a 16th century battlemented tower and two fine old doorways, one bricked up

13TH CENTURY    1400-1470    TUDOR

RENAISSANCE    QUEEN ANNE    GEORGIAN

An architrave is the moulded frame surrounding a door or window; a pediment, the decorated triangular or curved stone over a door or window; the initials and date of the owner-builder of a house and his wife refer to the house, not to the date of the marriage

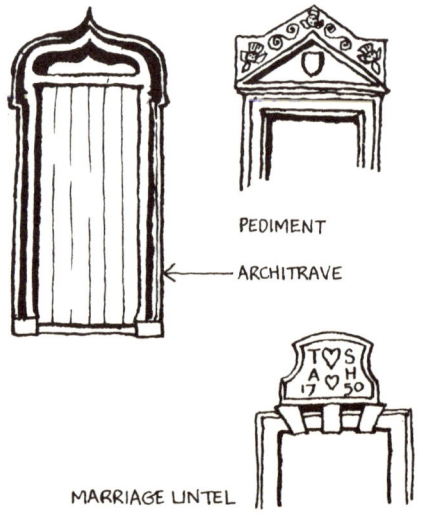

PEDIMENT

ARCHITRAVE

MARRIAGE LINTEL

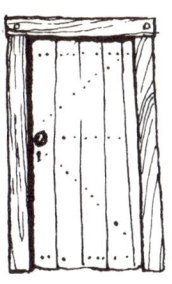

HEAVY WOOD FRAME

SUB-MEDIEVAL

TUDOR

REGENCY
1800-20

NOW

Doorway development

Look around

When you have noted the chief external features of the house, look for some of the following:

Decorations on stone and wood, particularly around doors and windows, eaves and gables, on gateposts and on stones set into walls.

Stairways. Are there any external stairways? Why might they be required? In some Scottish fishermen's houses the family lived on the first floor, the ground floor being used for storage.

Traces of an older building in the present one, e.g. a Tudor archway in a Georgian wall. The back of the house often presents more clues than the front.

A face in the wall, Fordham, Cambridge

A Tudor battlemented turret with coat of arms

*A cottage in Denton,
Northamptonshire, with date plaque
and trelliswork porch*

Unusual materials, e.g. an iron-framed house like that at Ditherington, Shropshire (dates from 1796).

Unusual shapes. There's a round house at Exmouth, Devon, and a hexagonal one at Snettisham, Norfolk. Can you add to these?

Porches. Wind porches date from 1550. Sedan chair porches can still be found.

A house with a 'round tower' and a 'spire'. Look for the style in Scotland. This one is near Lochearnhead, Perthshire

A sedan chair porch in Chester, Cheshire

Storage. Is there a basement or any provision for storage of goods or livestock? Look for metal covers over coal holes (which are excellent for rubbing). Some dog kennels and dovecots date from Tudor times.

Water supply. Is there a well or a pump?

Look for signs of an earlier water supply

Plaques commemorating famous people who have lived in, or have had associations with, the house.

Insurance marks which date from the time when each large insurance company had its own fire brigade.

Metal fittings such as a snuffer for a link boy's torch, an old gas lamp fitting, or a house anchor. These latter were used to give additional strength by joining the external walls to the house timbers. They are often ornate. Look also for dates and decoration on rainwater pipes, particularly near the eaves.

A dated cottage in Nayland, Suffolk

A lead fire insurance mark on a cottage near Cobham in Surrey, stamped 67954, the policy being issued in 1742

This house in Thaxted, Essex,
commemorates a distinguished
resident: the composer Gustav Holst

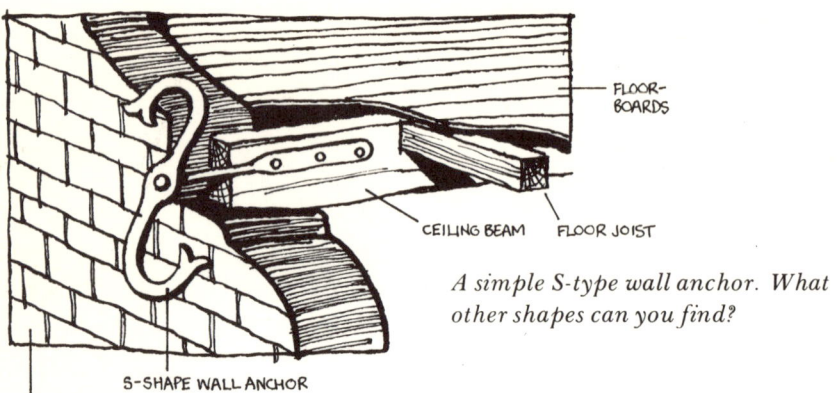

FLOOR-
BOARDS

CEILING BEAM   FLOOR JOIST

S-SHAPE WALL ANCHOR

OUTER WALL OF HOUSE

A simple S-type wall anchor. What other shapes can you find?

Outside features in iron

GAS LAMP
FROM
BRANCASTER
NORFOLK

LANCASHIRE WITCH
WEATHER VANE

Sundial on a Georgian house in Reepham, Norfolk

KNOCKER FROM
BATHAMPTON,
SOMERSET

LINK SNUFFER,
BATH, SOMERSET

A decorated water pipe on the Master Builder's House in Buckler's Hard, Hampshire . . .

. . . and a dated water pipe in Thaxted, Essex

Weathervanes and sundials.

The name of the house. Does this help us guess what it was originally used for?

'Malthouse' in Brockweir,
Gloucestershire. Although of earlier
ecclesiastical origin, this house was
once used for the making of malt
from barley

4 What to look for —inside

Many of the houses that you see you will be able to study only from the outside. Some old houses, however, have been converted into museums, and the list that follows will show you how detailed your study could be.

Rooms

What are the chief rooms called? Is there a solar (see p. 24), a withdrawing room, a buttery, a dairy or a pantry?

Kitchen

How old is the oven? Is there a bread oven? The bread oven might simply be a hole next to the main oven. It might be a separate unit with a cast-iron door. This type was filled with hot wood ash at night. In the morning the ash was cleared and bread baked in the still hot bricks. Is there a spit? How is it driven? (There may be a fan in the chimney breast which provides the power.) Is there a salt box in the wall near the fireplace? This was a small recess in which salt was stored. The heat kept the salt dry. Is there a bacon-curing chamber off the flue? Salting and smoking were the two main ways of preserving food before electricity and gas made refrigeration possible. In what other ways do the kitchen and the cooking utensils tell us something about the housekeeping of previous generations?

Fireplaces

Look at the fireback. Is it dated? Does it indicate anything (e.g. initials, crests) about past owners of the property? Are there any firedogs ('andirons')? These were designed to keep wood fires in place.

The walls

Interior wood linings were first introduced to keep out the damp and insulate against extremes of heat and cold. Look for:

Linenfold moulding.

Decorated moulding around doorways, on stairways and along beams supporting walls and ceilings. What wood is used? Greater detail is possible in pear and limewood than in oak.

Wainscotting—first introduced by Henry III in 1253 for his rooms at Windsor.

Wall paintings, painted panelling,

*A cast-iron decorated fireback,
dated 1645*

*A mediaeval fireplace with 'firedogs'
and a baking oven on one side*

wallpaper and tapestry. Some experts suggest that many eighteenth and nineteenth century houses were deliberately built facing north to prevent direct sunlight falling into the principal rooms, so reducing the fading of expensive fabrics and wall coverings.

Internal beams

Look for carpenters' numerals. The mediaeval carpenter probably cut the main timbers in his own workshop, and then carried them to the building site. For ease of erection the beams had to be numbered; and since Arabic numerals were not in common use Roman numerals were cut into the timbers. Some of the beams would be fitted in roof and ceiling, and would be worked from below. Since XI upside down might appear as IX and VI be easily confused with IV the following system developed. Notice how the 'fives' and 'tens' were simplified. Do not confuse these numerals with carpenters' marks: these indicate who cut and shaped the beam.

A king-post support to the roof timbers

Carpenters' numerals and marks

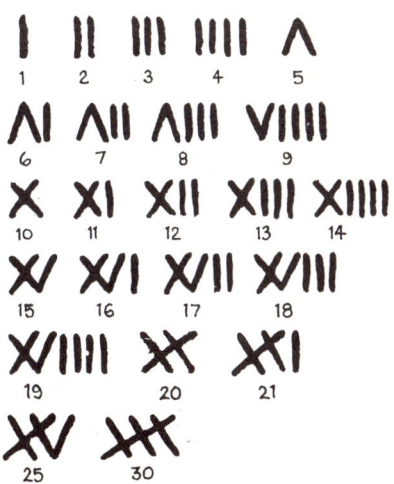

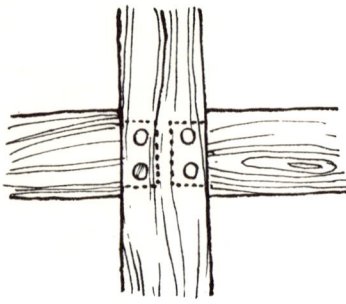

Wooden pegs used to joint beams

Jointing and pegging

How have the beams been joined?
Notice that metal was rarely used to
join wooden surfaces.

The floor

What material has been used for the
main rooms: trodden earth,
flagstones, tiles, lime ash, brick or
wood? The floorboard width may
help date the building. In late
mediaeval times the planks were 18
inches or more wide; in Georgian
times they varied between 12 and 14
inches.

The roof

Are there any rooms within the roof
space? How is the roof supported?

Ceilings

What material has been used? If
wooden, have they been carved; if
plaster, are they decorated?

The staircase

There are four principal types of
staircase. Which type does the house
have? Is there a 'dog gate' at the top
to keep animals from the bedrooms?
Some houses have a 'hanging'
staircase (e.g. The White House,
Aston Munslow, Shropshire) which is
a staircase supported entirely by the
external walls.

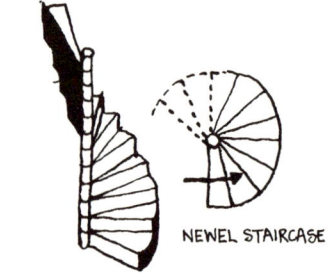

NEWEL STAIRCASE

*A newel staircase was inconvenient
because of the difference in the width
of the treads. A simple staircase was
really a ladder with the treads filled*

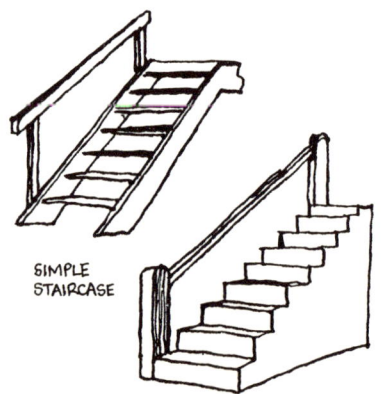

SIMPLE
STAIRCASE

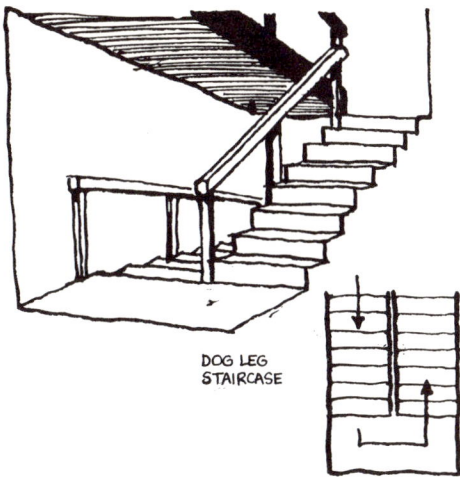

Furniture

Is there any unusual furniture on
display (e.g. four-poster beds,
stone-topped tables) or furniture
made by a famous craftsman such as
Thomas Chippendale (1718-99),
George Hepplewhite (d 1786),
Thomas Sheraton (1751-1806) or
Robert Gillow (d 1773)? Also look for
small stone cupboards cut into the
wall (an aumbry). A cupboard was
originally a flat board on which cups
were stored; only valuables would be
put in these 'wall safes'.

Internal doors

Is the shape the same as that of the
external doors? How are they hung?
Examine the fittings, particularly
hinges, locks, and keys.

Windows

Is there a window seat? How are the
windows made fast?

An aumbry or wall-cupboard

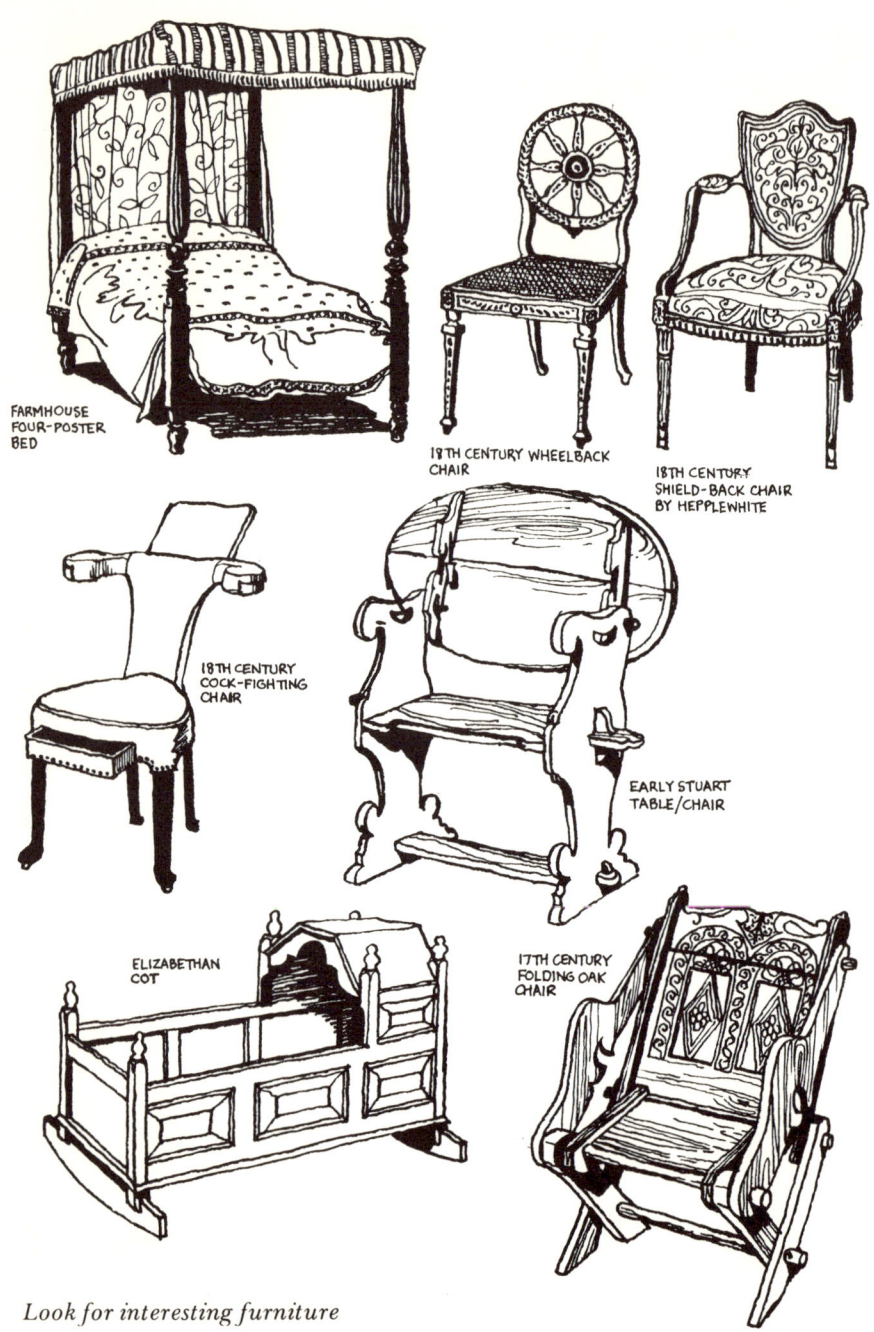

FARMHOUSE
FOUR-POSTER
BED

18TH CENTURY WHEELBACK
CHAIR

18TH CENTURY
SHIELD-BACK CHAIR
BY HEPPLEWHITE

18TH CENTURY
COCK-FIGHTING
CHAIR

EARLY STUART
TABLE/CHAIR

ELIZABETHAN
COT

17TH CENTURY
FOLDING OAK
CHAIR

Look for interesting furniture

5 Curiosities

Each house has a character of its own and it's worthwhile searching for the curious things that make it different from its neighbour. Here are some suggestions to help you when you begin to look for odd facts about any house you visit.

Boscobel Manor (near Wolverhampton) as it was when Charles II hid in it after the Battle of Worcester in September 1651

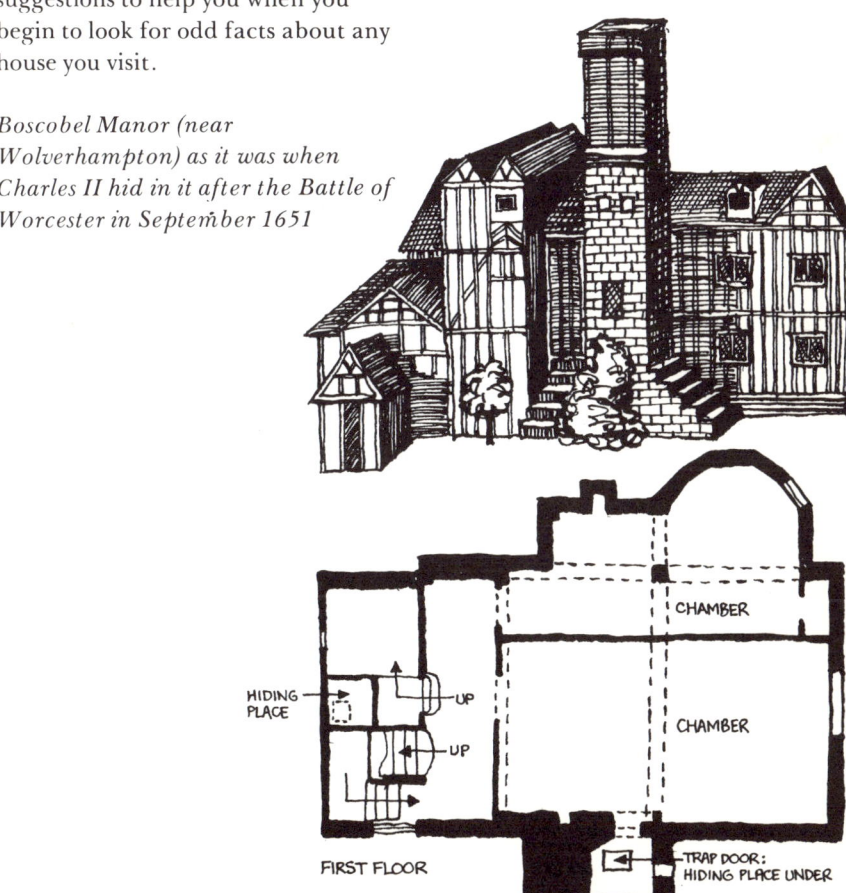

CHAMBER

HIDING PLACE

UP

UP

CHAMBER

FIRST FLOOR

TRAP DOOR: HIDING PLACE UNDER

Has the house any Royal associations? In the Royal House, Machynlleth, Montgomeryshire, Owen Glendower (1359-1415) held his first Parliament; the Court House, Long Crendon, Bucks, was given to Catherine of Aragon by Henry VIII.

Did any famous people once live in the house? The Washington family, for example, lived at Sulgrave Manor, Culworth, Northants; William Wordsworth at Dove Cottage, Grasmere, Westmorland; Charles Wesley in the City Road, London EC1; Robert Burns at Souter Johnnie's Cottage, Kirkoswald, Ayrshire. All of these are open to the public.

Was the house built as a memorial? There's a quaint stone house beneath the memorial to Sir William Wallace near Stirling, and a row of cottages at Tolpuddle, Dorset, to commemorate the six farm labourers who, in 1834, were transported to Australia because they formed a trade union.

The Priest's House by the church at Smallhythe, Kent; it was once the home of Ellen Terry the actress

Are there any 'priest's' or 'hiding' holes? Many of these date from the religious persecution of late Tudor and Stuart times. At Little Moreton Hall, Congleton, Cheshire, there are two secret chambers. One was 'built to be discovered'. The real hiding place was beneath the moat at the end of an underground passage.

Is there a chapel in the house—or is the house part of a church? Black Chapel (near Chelmsford, Essex) has the priest's house built into the church. At Wells in Somerset a whole row of houses was built in mediaeval times for the vicars-choral of the cathedral. Women were not allowed into these houses until quite recently.

Almshouses and a converted windmill in Thaxted, Essex

Is the house a 'hospital' (or almshouse)? Almshouses are to be found in most towns; many have a religious connection. In 1571 Robert Dudley established 'The Hospital and Chapel of St James' at Warwick for 'twelve poor and impotent persons'. The almshouse at Hambledon, near Canterbury, Kent, still receives a grant from a bequest that Henry II made on his way to pray at Becket's tomb. Try to arrange a visit when the almshouses are open to the public. The elderly folk are usually full of stories and legends about their founder. Ask about the customs they have to observe, and their ceremonial dress. At Castle Rising, Norfolk, it consists of red cloak, steeple hat, and the Howard Badge (Henry Howard, Earl of Northamptonshire).

Is the house in an unexpected place? For example, is the house on a bridge? There's a mediaeval bridge in Lincoln that carries a row of houses, and a house on a bridge at Ambleside (Westmorland). Legend has it that this was built over water by a Scotsman to prevent his having to pay ground rent!

Has the building always been a house? Look for the following: oast houses, houses in windmills, watermills, railway stations and even signal boxes. At Ixworth in Suffolk a house was built over the ruined abbey and incorporates the night stair (or slyp) that led from the dormitory to the church.

Was the house built for a specific purpose? E.g. as a toll house, a lock keeper's house, a gate house to a park or a stately home.

Are there any strange stories associated with the house? A heart-shaped box was found in Erwarton House, Suffolk, in 1836. Did it contain the heart of Anne Boleyn, executed by Henry VIII in 1536? How many people *were* executed at Court House, Ruthin, Denbighshire? Built in 1404, this house had a gallows attached to it. There is still a gibbet projecting from the roof! And ghosts? Squire Butler, a white lady, a squirrel and a hare, together with a disembodied head and a clanking chain, are said to haunt Barnwall Abbey House, Cambridge. On a happier note, what evidence is there that King John of France was 'entertained' in French Row, Rye, Sussex, after he had lost the Battle of Poitiers in 1356?

Is there a herb garden? Herbs were used to give flavour to food and as a medicine. Look for the following: balm, basil, bay, bergamot, borage (or bugloss), chamomile, chervil, chives, clary, coltsfoot, coriander, dill, dittany, fennel, foxglove, garlic, horseradish, hyssop, jessop, knapweed, lavender, lovage, marjoram, mint, myrtle, orris, parsley, pellitory, poppy, rosemary, rue, sage (red and common), savory, sorrel, tansy, tarragon, thyme, verbena, woad, wormwood. You might make a collection of herbal recipes — but don't experiment with them on yourself or your family!

6 Some things to do

1 Recording the things you have found can be very rewarding, but it can become a bore if you try to note every fact that you have discovered. Be selective. Choose one or two things about each house you visit and make detailed notes only on the subject of your choice (e.g. windows and doorways; carving and decoration; associations; curiosities).

2 Have a note pad, a pencil (and a sharpener) and a board to rest on. Several quick sketches that can be developed later will be more worthwhile to you than one time-consuming drawing.

3 Use a tape recorder and a camera whenever practical. A tape is likely to be more accurate than your notes and a photograph more detailed than your drawings.

4 Mount your material in a loose-leaf folder. This will enable you to alter the layout and content of your study as it develops.

5 Experiment in layout. Is it best to show developments you have noted in an historical sequence or county by county (or town by town)?

6 Buy postcards and booklets of the places you visit and incorporate them into your collection.

7 Have any other buildings in the area links with the houses you have studied, e.g. are previous owners buried in the local church, do paintings of them hang in the local museum?

8 Are there any sketches of the house as it once was? Look for these in museums, antique shops and old guide books. Old maps will help here, particularly if they are detailed enough to show outbuildings that might no longer exist.

9 Make your own survey — the chart indicates the sort of information to record.

House survey no. 17 **Date** May 1973 **Situation** Chambercombe, Ilfracombe, Devon
Name or street no. Chambercombe Manor

EXTERNAL

Materials used—
Walls: Local stone? Whitewashed.
Roof: Tiles. Gabled, two levels.
Chimneys: Two stacks on external walls, another through roof.
Doors: Entrance door oak—studded with bolts.
Windows: Dormer in roof. Small panes, look like Renaissance, but not sure.

INTERNAL

Rooms: Ground floor: Hall, Chapel, Kitchen, Dairy. First floor: Four bedrooms and a dressing room. No basement, but there was an internal court.

Interesting features: Floor of lime ash (sand/lime/ash mixed with cider, trampled in with hobnail boots). I liked the tiny chapel (10 ft. x 6 ft.)
There was a Gothic and a Tudor door—both wooden.

Furniture/fittings: Several 4-poster beds, one of yew. Some Chippendale and a Cromwellian table with barley-twist legs.
Saw a lace-maker's lamp →
There's also a Victorian bedroom with a prayer-chair.

GOTHIC DOOR

CHAPEL

Hour glass

MEDIEVAL WINDOW

Finishes: Plaster ceiling in main bedroom with a Tudor rose

Legends/historical associations: Lady Jane Grey stayed in the house. Haunted room— blocked up and has no windows. In 1765 skeleton of a woman was found, apparently a victim of shipwreckers, off Hele Beach.
There's said to be a secret passage from the coast to the house.
Chambercombe appears in Domesday Book, and there's a deed on views dated 1701.

Reliable features for dating the building:
Lots of dated fittings (like firebacks), ceilings, thickness of walls, dovecote under eaves.
Very wide floorboards on first floor. (18"?)

CENTRE COURTYARD

If you are lucky enough to find any old drawings or photographs of the houses you are studying, take a photograph from the same angle and see how things have changed.

In the present-day picture of Brockweir on the River Wye, the whole row of cottages on the right has disappeared to make way for a lay-by

7 Houses and people

Some houses to visit

Jane Austen: Chawton, Alton, Hampshire

Sir James Barrie: Barrie's Birthplace, Kirriemuir, Aberdeen

The Brontës: Parsonage Museum, Haworth, Yorkshire and Oakwell Hall, Batley, Yorkshire

Robert Burns: Burns Cottage, Alloway, Ayrshire

Thomas Carlyle: Carlyle House, Cheyne Row, London, S.W.3

Charles II: Moseley Old Hall, Wolverhampton, Staffs and Boscobel House, Shifnal, Shropshire

Samuel Taylor Coleridge: Coleridge Cottage, Nether Stowey, Somerset

Oliver Cromwell: Chavenage, Chetbury, Gloucestershire

Lord Darnley: Temple Newsam, Leeds, Yorkshire

Charles Darwin: Downe House, Downe, Kent

Charles Dickens: Bleak House, Broadstairs, Kent and 48 Doughty Street, London, W.C.1

Benjamin Disraeli: Hughenden Manor, High Wycombe, Buckinghamshire

Thomas Gainsborough: Gainsborough House, Sudbury, Suffolk

Sir Richard Grenville: Buckland Abbey, Nr Plymouth, Devon

Thomas Hardy: Hardy's Cottage, Higher Beckhampton, Dorset

William Hogarth: Hogarth House, Chiswick, London

Rudyard Kipling: Batemans, Burwash, Sussex

T. E. Lawrence (of Arabia): Cloudshill, Nr Wareham, Dorset

Mary Queen of Scots: Traquair House, Inner Leithen, Peeblesshire

William Morris: Kelmscott Manor, Nr Lechlade, Gloucestershire

Sir Alfred Munnings: Castle House, Dedham, Essex

Sir Isaac Newton: Woolthorpe Manor, Nr Grantham, Lincolnshire

Florence Nightingale: Claydon House, Claydon, Nr Winslow, Buckinghamshire

William Shakespeare: The Shakespeare Properties, Stratford-on-Avon, Warwickshire

Laurence Sterne: Shandy Hall, Coxwold, Yorkshire

Ellen Terry: Smallhythe Place, Tenterden, Kent

George Washington: Sulgrave Manor, Banbury, Oxfordshire

Charles and John Wesley: The Old Rectory, Epworth, Lincolnshire

and Buckland Rectory, Nr Broadway, Gloucestershire and Wesley's House, City Road, London, E.C.1
William Wilberforce: Wilberforce House, Kingston-upon-Hull, Yorkshire

James Wolfe: Quebec House, Westerham, Kent
William Wordsworth: Rydal Mount, Ambleside, Westmorland and Wordsworth House, Cockermouth, Cumberland